THE DAILY SPARK PLUG

DIVINE REVELATIONS

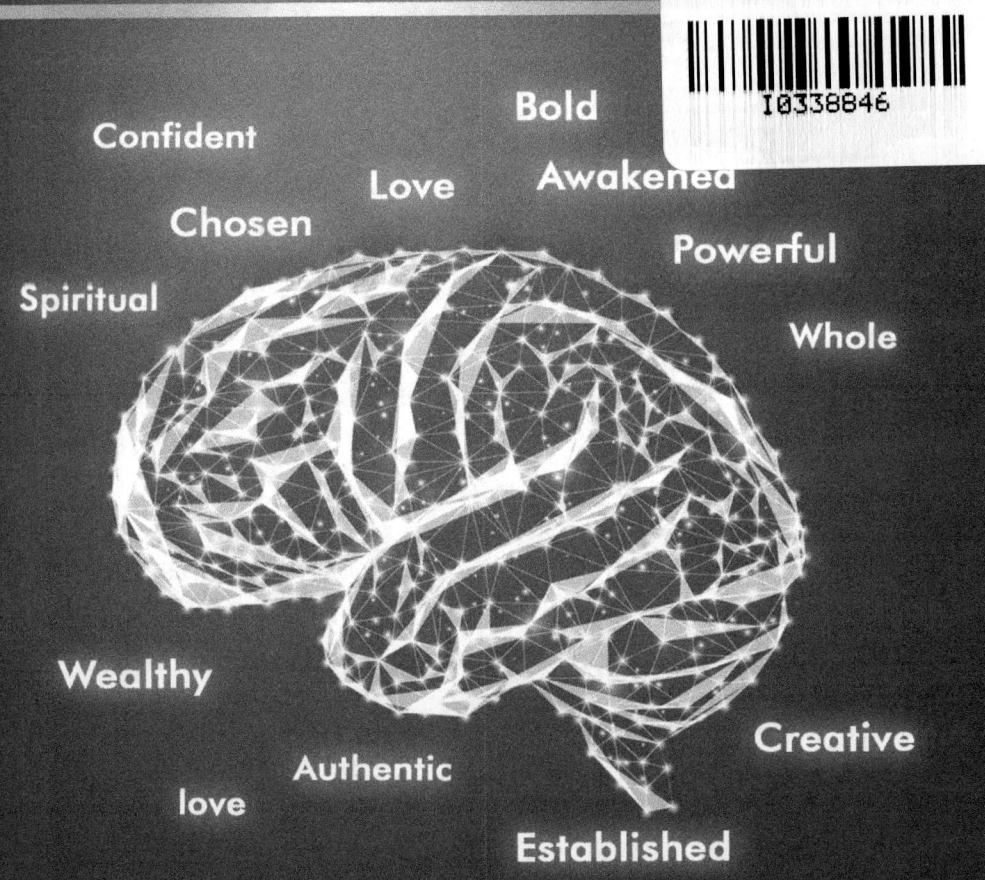

Confident
Bold
Love
Awakened
Chosen
Powerful
Spiritual
Whole
Wealthy
Creative
Authentic
love
Established

TIFFANY EALY

Copy Right, 2021 by TESPEAKS

All rights are reserved. This book or any portion of this book may not be reproduced without written permission from the author, except for brief quotations that may be used in a book review.

First Printing, 2021 www.tiffanyealyspeaks@gmail.com

TE Speaks, LLC

PO Box 1192

Fresno, TX 77545

Prophetic Word

Contents

INTRO: Get Ready 6
I AM 8
DAY 1: Jewel Power 11
DAY 2: Speak Life 13
DAY 3: Tradition/Obedience 15
DAY 4: Operate From The Seat 17
DAY 5: You Are Valuable 19
DAY 6: One Word 21
DAY 7: Miracle Season 23
DAY 8: Your Next 25
DAILY SPARK PLUG: Chosen Jewel 26
DAY 9: Raw To Manifestation 28
DAY 10: The Mechanic 76
DAY 11: Adjust Your Now 32
DAY 12: Consultant 34
DAY 13: Exodus 36
DAY 14: Momentum Of Heaven 38
DAILY SPARK PLUG: Look Ahead 39
DAY 15: The Cleaner 41
DAY 16: Center 43

DAY 17: ANGELS ON ASSIGNMENT 45
DAY 18: THE WAR 47
DAY 19: SOAR 49
DAILY SPARK PLUG: LOOK AHEAD 50
DAY 20: CHOSEN 52
DAY 21: COME BACK 54
DAILY SPARK PLUG: LOOK AHEAD 55
DAY 22: PRUNING 57
DAY 23: WE ARE COVERED 59
DAY 24: THE MOUNTAIN 61
DAY 25: CHANGE IS HERE 63
DAILY SPARK PLUG: WORDS HAVE POWER 64
DAY 26: DRY BONES 66
DAY 27: BEAUTY IN THE PAIN 68
DAY 28: THE BLESSING 70
DAILY SPARK PLUG: PAIN TO PURPOSE 71
DAY 29: FORGIVENESS IS IMPT. 73
DAY 30: RE-ROUTED 75
DAILY SPARK PLUG: SOWING 76
PRAYER TO IGNITE **77**

Intro

Get Ready

Get ready to soar to new heights, and new directions. The stretching and increase comes from the father above. You must activate the faith that is within. You already have a measure of faith, but you must walk in it. The power of God shall be seen over your life as you read ahead and study my word. Sometimes, you may not know what direction to follow. Look to me, neither to the left nor to the right, but look ahead and journey forth. Your blessing is in front of you. You can't figure everything out by yourself. I made you and I know where you are going. I know the steps ahead and I know your purpose. In everything you do, give it to me and pray. When you access me, I will give you my touch. My touch is what makes the impossible possible. I am the only way, and no one can lead you to my plans but me. I am multi-faceted and I made you that way as well. Review my word, and speak life over your day, business, and family. Now that you are ready to move forward, get ready because it is now time to release the blessing over your life. The blessing that belongs to you shall be seen by you and it shall prevail.

Prophetic Word

I AM

I am created by God, the Elohim. I am wonderfully made, and more than enough. The more than enough created me for a purpose and with a divine destiny. The fullness of purpose and the true manifestation of purpose shall prevail. I shall operate from the origin and the seat of Heaven. The momentum of Heaven shall invade the Earth. I shall operate and have thoughts of the perfect plans and blueprints of Heaven. I am a manifestation of Yahweh on Earth. I live to glorify the Father. I shall be made whole and one with the true identity of whom I am called to be. I speak, the fullness of potential shall manifest and come forth. The I AM, is the way-maker and promise-keeper, and all that I am… I call forth from Heaven to Earth. I am exactly who the Father created me to be from the beginning of time. The fullness of the manifestation of Elohim lives in me. I am one with the true identity of Christ. All those assigned to me shall be touched and changed, because I A<u>M</u> one with the I AM.

"The secret of success is accessing your true identity and learning to walk in your truth, if you do not know your truth, you will abuse it and downgrade your true worth!"

- Tiffany Ealy

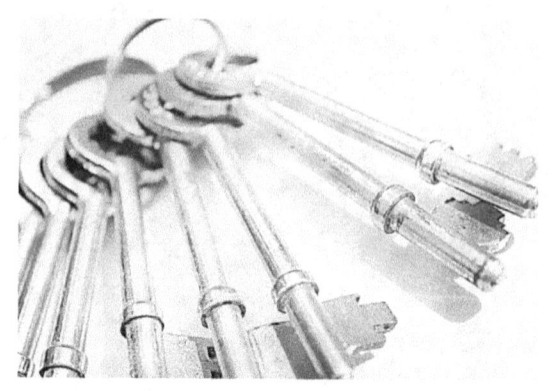

Spiritual Key 1

Your Identity Is Important

Greetings, sons and daughters of the king, you were born with a purpose from above. You can only become fully awake to your true self when you know your identity. You truly owe it to yourself... to walk in the assignment you are called to walk in. You owe it to yourself; to see how wonderful and powerful you truly are. You have an assignment and people attached to your purpose that need what you have. Make an impact today, and pray and ask the Father, the creator, Elohim who He created you to become. Go forth into your true purpose, and live from your true origin of Heaven.

Day 1

Jewel Power

Each of us is created in the image and likeness of the Father, Elohim. Elohim means creator... He is the one who created all and created all that is. Our image can be seen by the physical eye, but the outer appearance is not who we truly are. It is a shell that we wear, while we are on Earth. The true identity of who we are comes from within. We must have the Holy Spirit, who is our guide and comforter. Our true identity operates from within the Spirit realm, and when we are connected to the spirit, we can be guided and walk from the true core of who we were created to be. Without the Spirit, we can only walk in partial identity. When we are truly aware of our position and how special and unique we are, we can go forth in boldness to walk in our God-given assignment. We must know fully who we are, so we can operate fully as we were created. Life brings many ups and downs, but when we know who we are, we can't be moved. Many times, we try and impress man, but we must look to our Father who created us. We have promises and a future that is already stored up for us waiting to be released by the Father. Often times, man doesn't even know what the Father has placed inside of us. We must each day, look to the Father to fulfill our assignment. When we leave this Earth, and have walked in our Jewel Power, we can fully say that we poured out everything within, and touched many lives for His glory.

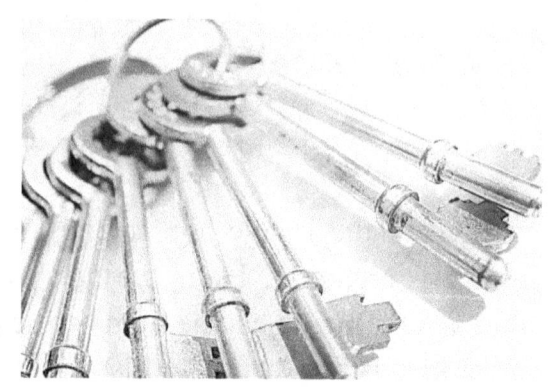

Spiritual Key 2
Fine-Tune Your Mind

Fine-Tune Your Mind and know the promises of God. Walk in the right mind-set daily where you fine-tune your thoughts to the thoughts above. Think about what you are thinking about. Make sure that your thoughts line up with the word. Decree, believe, trust, expect and move forward. Leave behind the past because you are moving in now and your future is greater.

Day 2

Speak Life

Our mouths have the power within to speak life or death. Today, we need to decide to think before we speak. Just like the Elohim that created the Earth by His words. We have the power to create with our words. I remember my Great Aunt speaking life over her plants and nurturing them with love. She certainly had a green thumb with plants. Just like she spoke and fed the plants, we need to feed our spirits within. Our mouths have a voice to speak to objects, people and atmospheres to create and bring life. Even things that are in a dead position, we have the power to bring them back to life with our words. Our words have power to speak and it shall be. We also have power to speak to the mountains or storms in our life and declare them successful. We can change our position with our words. Our words should always line up with God's word and what we want to see. Our complaining is only hindering us from moving ahead. When we speak life and not death, we are adjusting our situation, so it lines up with God's divine word. We are kingdom beings and as citizens of the kingdom, our words activate the blessing. God is able to command the angels above to go to work on our behalf. Today, move forward in faith and decree life and speak it until you see the manifestation of your prayers. In due season, you will see the manifestation of His power in your life.

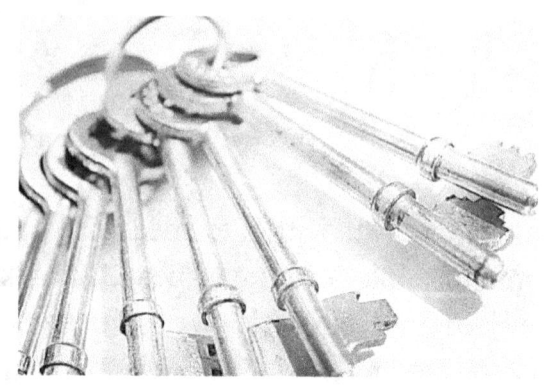

Spiritual Key 3

Obedience Is Key

Some traditions are good and if we are not careful some traditions can hold us back. The true key to move ahead in who God called us to be is to break free of any traditions, and religion holding us back. We must walk in obedience to God's will for our life. Obedience to the father is key in walking in our Purpose and walking in the belief system of the Kingdom and not man.

Day 3

Tradition/Obedience

There are many traditions that our parents did because that is what their parents did. It is important for us to research and know what traditions that do not serve us, and would hold us back in bondage. For example, eating black-eyed peas for New Year's Day. Do we truly understand why and where this tradition started? This tradition started because this was the staple eaten by the soldiers during the cold season, and there was also leftovers for the slaves. Our family chooses to eat our favorite meal, and my husband as the head of our household sows a first-fruit seed into each of us. This is a tradition that our family chooses to follow and we know that blessings shall flow during the year. We want to start our New Year being obedient and sowing seeds that shall produce a harvest. God wants us to be obedient to what He is telling us to do, and apply His wisdom, so we can have great success. His plans are true and they can't be undone. We must stand and be obedient to the Father, and we know we will have great success. We are disciples of God meant to bring forth His glory. Obedience is always key for us walking in purpose. We are blood line breakers, atmosphere changers, and created to touch lives for the kingdom. We must create traditions that we understand and that line up with God's plan and purpose for our lives.

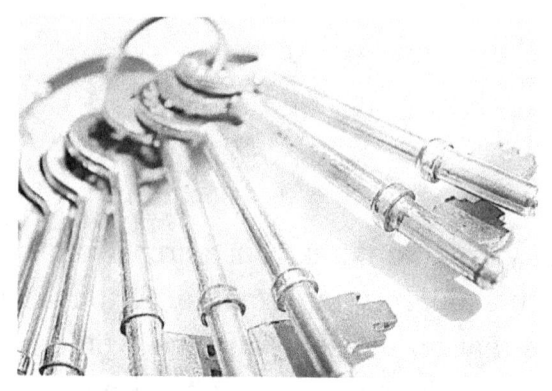

Spiritual Key 4
Wisdom

We receive wisdom from the Holy Spirit. The Holy Spirit operates as our guide, comforter, and teacher. We are directed in the direction we should go by the Spirit that lives within. Wisdom brings forth clarity and insight. We can make sound decisions, because wisdom guides us to make decisions and operate in the knowing of God. The wisdom of God produces fruit and brings forth desired blessings.

Day 4

Operate From The Seat

God's word says that we are seated in Heavenly places. That means that we operate with full access from Heaven to Earth. We are seated with the Father in the throne room, and we can operate to pull down things from Heaven to bring forth onto Earth. We were created for a purpose and to operate in that purpose from our origin and seat. When we operate from our reserved seated position, we operate from a position of authority, creativity, and

and abundance. We operate in a position that produces the promise. We are unable to operate from the seat without faith and wisdom of God. Our name is already written in the books of Heaven, and we have treasures that are waiting to be unlocked. We are uniquely made with a purpose, to operate fully in our identity and purpose that is only true to us. When we operate in authenticity and show up fully that we have power. Our skill will create the momentum and the gifts will open up. We will produce a return when we operate from our seat, and doors will swing open. The treasures within are brought down from Heaven, and your Jewel now operates fully. Today, ask for wisdom that your thoughts will begin to line up with the plans of Heaven, and you can operate from the prepared place. The Father has anointed this time— that Heaven may invade and manifestation shall come forth. This is your appointed time to fill your seat and possess the territory.

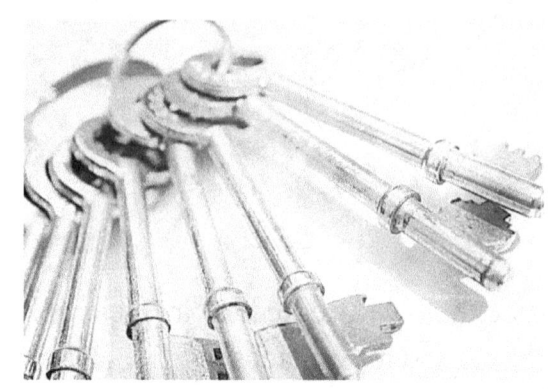

Spiritual Key 5

Sowing Produces the Harvest

When you sow and give back into you are creating more than enough. As we give, we shall receive. It is a law that the more that we give, the more we shall receive back. When we give; we open up the doors, wells for our harvest to come back to us. We should sow into others, sow into others that are doing what you want to do. It is important to sow into your purpose and future. Sow love, give time, and give monetarily into the things you believe in. In due season, you shall receive back, because you serve the God of more than enough.

Day 5

You Are Valuable

When you look at the outside of your home, you see the exterior only. The true value of your home is within the inside. The outside flowers and color make the exterior nice, and a pleasure to look at. The inside is where the true value is found, and the treasures. We are valuable as sons and daughters, and our value is within. The more we add and upgrade our homes, the more value within. This is true to us as well. When we pray, fast, and read the word, and walk in purpose, we unlock our value. Our true value comes from our walking in purpose and from the treasures within. Our value comes from operating from our seat and the treasures of Heaven. You are made to operate from your Jewel, your money-maker. Your Jewel creates opportunities and open doors. When you operate from the origin, you are operating from the gifts and your skills shall bring forth streams. You are one step, one word, one shift away from the open doors, open wells, and your walk in abundance. Keep moving ahead, keep being obedient, and keep trusting in His word. God's plans for your life shall prevail and shall bring forth more than enough. You are valued by God and your value shall bring forth abundance and a harvest.

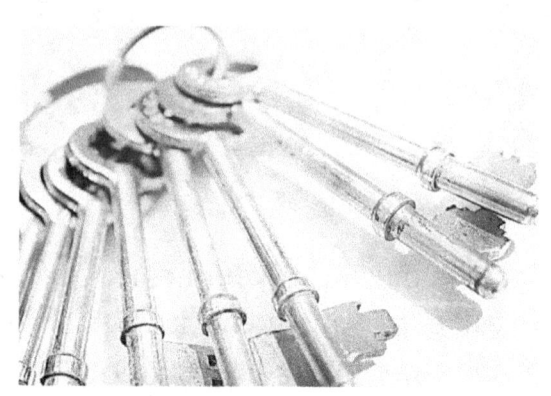

Spiritual Key 6

Expect & Believe

Expect that God will do what He said He would do in your life. We should live elevated, because we are a part of the kingdom. We must think big, activate our minds to trust God and get rid of doubt. My former Apostle Alice S. Martin always said "Treat doubt like dope and stay away." We must place our expectations in the things above and not in man. When we believe and activate faith, we will see the manifestations of our prayers.

Day 6

One Word

We always have a solution to our problems. In **(Psalm 97:5)**, it says that when we speak to the mountains it shall melt like wax before the Lord and Earth. Our true answer is our Father, He is our Exodus. He is available 24/7 for consulting and prayer. God can place a divine word, moment, a person, or a divine touch in your life that will change your momentum to align with His plans. God knows exactly how to get your attention. He does give us free will to decide for ourselves. If we know better, we will walk in obedience and go forward in His plans, because His plans are perfect and shall come to pass. One moment, we may walk in the wilderness, and then after one word or confirmation God can bring us to the fore-front. You are one-step, one-word, and one-movement away from your answer. Keep moving ahead and stay grounded in the momentum of God Stay in position and rooted in His word. Your shift starts within your mind and your mouth. Start declaring what you want to see, and it shall come to pass. Everything that you are going through will not be wasted, but it shall be used for His glory. Use the pain, and help to bring others out, and God will get the glory. Everything you are going through is not so you will fail, but so you will stand and help someone else. Your shift is here, and your word shall come forth in due time.

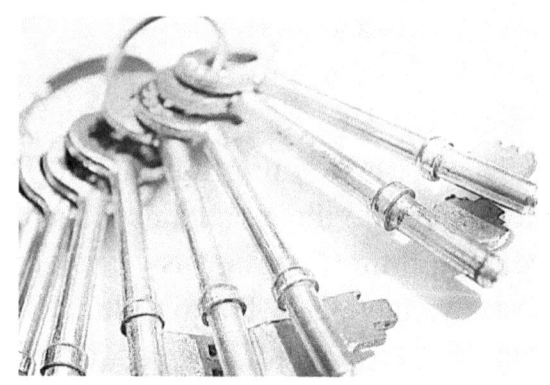

Spiritual Key 7

Love

Love is one of the greatest acts that the Father cares about. We exist to give love and help those in need. The Father wants us to care about what He loves. Today, show acts of kindness and love, we are meant to be a light in dim places and the love we show is a reflection of the Father within.

Day 7

Miracle Season

Christmas time is a season that we look forward to, in which, we celebrate the existence of Jesus Christ. It is a time where we sow into those in need, and we are Christ's angels on Earth. Our Father is a wonder that can't be explained. His splendor and glory is beyond words. He wants our lights to shine not only during Christmas, but daily. When our lights are dim, He always sends someone to help us recharge and provides us with strength. The light that we need is always through the Father. No one, can dim our light, unless we let them. The Father's presence is all we need. He is available to bring His perfect plans to pass in our lives. There is a movie, in which, a non-profit brought the 12-days of miracles to a town. This town looked forward to the daily blessings, and they wrote down there Christmas wishes. The Christmas wishes were always received, but it was a mystery how the blessings came to pass. Our Father is the creator that wants to bring every promise to our lives. When we seek Him, and reflect on who He is, we can receive and walk in divine miracles. What a blessing it is to see faces light up when they receive a blessing they have prayed for. Every day, seek to give love and show acts of kindness, because you are someone's miracle.

I declare that my promises shall come to pass now, doors are open and I receive elevation in every area of my life.

Day 8

Your Next

As a child, I enjoyed watching the show… the Price is Right. We responded like our name had just been called to come forward. The excitement of the audience when their names were called was excitement and dancing. That is how our Father wants us to act when we pray. He wants us to get excited about our blessing and prepare for the blessing. He wants us to know that our blessing is not for the future, but it is for now. Get into an anticipation that the Father has just called your name. Write your perfect plans down, and goals. Consult the Father for wisdom regarding what you have prayed for. The Father has already written down every blessing in your book in Heaven. He knows just how to provide you with the promises. You are next in line, get ready, keep praying, keep believing, keep sowing, and prepare as if it is already done. The blessing may not come how you think and when, but it is ready to be released. The Father is sure to bring your blessing to pass. Your situation can change at a moment's notice, one touch can place you from the bottom to the top. Your blessing is ready to be released, get prepared for the release. You are the next recipient and your name is being called now. You shall receive not just a blessing but more than you thought possible. Shout! It is your time right now.

Daily Spark Plug

Chosen Jewel

You are a chosen Jewel; chosen to do great things. Your true value lies within. You are fully whole when you walk and operate from your seat above. You owe it to yourself... to see your true value, someone needs what you have!

I decree that everything that belongs to me shall manifest and come to pass in my life!

Day 9

Raw to Manifestation

There is a plate before you that has bacon, eggs, sausage, and bread, and everything is not cooked. The plate is no good to you, because it is in a raw state. The food is useless to you, unless it is cooked. Once the breakfast is cooked, you can enjoy a delicious meal that feeds your stomach. In our raw state, we are no good to help others. We have baggage like rejection, unforgiveness, worry, doubt, and other things that we carry within us. We can't be effective to help others, until we are healed and whole. The Father must clean us and mold us, and prepare us to operate from our kingdom origin. We must read the word and rehearse the word. We must pray and fast, so that we can be cleansed and renew our minds daily. After we unclog the things that doesn't serve us, then we can serve others. God wants us to operate in our full potential that He has already equipped us to operate in. We must operate from a place of true identity to fully reach the top of our mountain (destiny). We must have the revelation and wisdom of the Holy Spirit to know who we are, and also know who our Father created us to be. Lastly, we must be obedient and willing to say yes to our destiny. Life is a journey and as long quick and easy. We must be willing to take the full journey, so we can see the manifestation of destiny in our lives. The manifestation of destiny in our lives opens us up to reach and touch lives and bring glory to the Father. As long as we are here, there is more for us to do, so that the manifestation of the Father's glory shall shine forth.

Lord, we decree that we are healed and made whole to operate in the fullness of your divine assignment today!

Day 10

The Mechanic

When your car is not functioning correctly, you call a mechanic. The mechanic does an overhaul to see the problem. When we have an issue and going through the storm, we must call the Father. The Father is our full service mechanic. He is the I AM. He is everything we need. He knows our issue, and also knows how to fix it, and the root cause. He does a complement rearrangement on the inside. He unclogs all the areas that are stopped up. He delivers us from ourselves and the things that mean us no good. He is the Exodus (The Answer) the true mechanic. He created us in His image and liking. He can heal our insecurities, and our discouragement. He can adjust our current situation and bring us to a place of peace and rest in Him. He renews us like the eagles and brings the right things in our pathway. He can close doors and open doors at the blink of an eye. He is more than enough, and He establishes more than enough within us. Each day is a gift from God. We must pray and seek our Father when we need a spark from the mechanic. Life throws us many balls that can dim our spark. When we feel like we are not operating in tune with our Father, we must pray, fast, and seek His wisdom. The mechanic knows how to heal every wall within, He is the creator and the divine healer. Our full service mechanic stays available and is always ready to provide us with His services. Call on Him, and you won't be disappointed.

Lord, we decree that right now, the blessings shall flow freely and manifest in our lives!

Day 11

Adjust Your Now

Many of us come to a crossroad in life, and we feel stuck. We are unsure what our next move should be, or where we are headed. We feel like we should be further along than we are. Rest assured, that the Father knows exactly where you are and He can place you where you need to be. He wants to adjust your current moment to match His plans for your life. He wants you to begin to walk in the momentum of Heaven, and stretch your capacity to match Heaven. He wants us to unlock Heaven in our lives and walk in destiny. When we unlock destiny, we can then begin to understand how special and powerful we are to the Father. God is able to change your path from wilderness to now at a moment's notice. You must know that every trial is a part of purpose. The Father will use it for His glory, and your testimony is for others. He will guide us and show us the way. He knows how to catapult us and advance us to now. God is a Father of now. He wants us to be blessednow. He wants us to win now. He wants to use us now, so we can bless others. It is now time for us to walk in true purpose, and our true identity. Only when we begin to know our true identity can we be fully powerful and operate in the power and manifestation of now.

Lord, we decree that your perfect plans and design for our lives shall manifest perfectly and come to pass.

Day 12

Consultant

Often times, we think about how we think our lives should look. We don't think about asking God to show us how He sees our life, and a glimpse of our promises. We develop our prayers based on our wants mostly and not our needs. We pray small prayers and not big prayers. Have you prayed for the revelation, knowledge of God's plan. His plans are perfect, and when we know His plan, it is only Plan A. His plans are true and shall prevail and come forth. We have dreams that He has given us that lie dormant. We have the authority to speak to our dead dreams, so they can live again. Our Father wants the best for us, and He wants us to consult and look to Him. He wants us to walk in the kingdom favor and blessings. All the kingdom attributes are good and wonderful. Healing, wealth, goodness, love, peace and abundance are all part of the kingdom. We have access to the greatest consultant with our blueprint on hand. When we feel that we are stuck and need help, we should access our consultant. He knows all, and has perfect information. Each day, we should have an expectation to operate fully aware of the Father's plan. Consult our Elohim, for clarity and instruction, because the only blueprint is in His hands. We have a full service consultant that is available to speak with us daily, all we have to do is call on Him. He wants each of us to make Him priority in our lives.

I decree, Lord that you are our Exodus, and we walk in wholeness, and we are an Exodus for those assigned to us.

Day 13

Exodus

The Father is everything you need, and is the answer to all. He is a different thing to each of us depending on our needs. He is the I Am. He is the Exodus (The Answer) He is the creator of all that is, and all that was created. He is the beginning and the end. He delivers, saves, heals, prepares and protects us. He is the truth, and His plans for us are perfect. He is our lifter, and He holds us in His hands. When we need an answer, He is there to help us who seek Him. He is the only answer that can bring us to a place of wholeness. Our Father is able to remove the old debris, hurts, pains, and rejection and bring forth new. He is the Father of more than enough, and He creates the enough in us. The answer is always through the Father. He knows all our needs and He is faithful to bring them forth. He does give us a choice to choose Him, or the world. He will provide us with ways to escape our emotions, financial problems, and insecurities. He provides a way for our exit in order to operate in the fullness of His creation. The Father has created us as vessels to be used by Him. He has created us to be the answer for those assigned to our lives. We are called to change lives, and be the answer to those in need. The Exodus who lives in us gives us power and authority to bring forth light in this world. The Lord shall be your Exodus, and you shall be an Exodus and an answer as well.

Lord, we decree that the momentum of Heaven is brought down to Earth and activated in our life!

Day 14

Momentum of Heaven

As kids, most of us put a puzzle together, and it came with many pieces. You had to figure out what pieces fit together to complete the puzzle. Our life has many pieces that fit together to create our true destiny. Each time we unlock a part of purpose, we have added to our puzzle. Each piece of the puzzle can be seen as a piece of destiny. We must continue to move forward and seek God's perfect plan in order to obtain our next piece. Each puzzle piece is a chapter in our story. Our story is not complete, until we leave this Earth. The momentum of Heaven to be fully engaged in our destiny comes from Heaven. We must access the Father and thirst for His living waters. Inside of us are wells of treasures that have to be unlocked and discovered by us. We must have the wisdom and insight through the spirit to know who we are and shall become. Walking in the presence of God leads us to quest for more. Our assignment is to bring Him glory and change the lives assigned to us. Someone connected to us are waiting for us to answer their prayers. Someone needs us to complete the next puzzle piece, so there life can be changed. Keep pushing ahead in the momentum of Heaven, stay grounded and rooted in love. The momentum of Heaven operates in now. Your words create the atmosphere around you and activates your life. Stay in His presence expecting abundance and commanding the blessing.

Daily Spark Plug

Look Ahead

In life you will make many mistakes, Mistakes teach us what not to do. Dust off and get back up. Trust in the Father's plan, and the Holy Spirit is our guide and comforter. We are God's sheep and He wants the best for us. Everything in our life will work for our good in the end! Look ahead, your future is Big!

Prayers and Reflections

Lord, may you cleanse us from the inside out, and may you renew our minds to reflect your plans and truths.

Day 15

The Cleaner

Our bodies inside have stinky stuff, toxins, and bacteria within. The hurt, pains, worries, also attach to us as baggage and cause sickness and heartaches. We become clogged and can't operate fully. Our spirit must be cleansed by fasting and praying. Fasting allows us to release the old and be filled and restored. It unclogs us to be able to think with clarity, insight, and wisdom. We must also read the word and access The Cleaner. Our Father is the cleaner and the restorer. He can heal us of our insecurities and remove all the rejection and baggage within. Just a touch from Him is all we need. Once the cleaner heals us, we must continue to renew our minds with His word and rehearse the word. Our bodies carry a load daily and life enters our pathway. We will have problems, but we must speak the word and trust in the Father. We must not let our problems consume our lives. The Father allows us to be cleansed and cast all our cares upon Him. The cleaner is able to clean our pipes when we fast, and we ask for His help. We must continue to remain in His presence and seek after Him for more. The cleaner is able to bring us back to a state of wholeness; if we let Him in.

Prayers and Reflections

Lord, we make you first in our lives, and we ask for your leading, and that our thought line up with your agenda and plans.

Day 16

Center

This Earth was formed and a foundation was built by our Father. It was spoken into existence— the Father is the center of the foundation of the Earth and our existence. Our Father should always be the source of our agenda for the day. I am not truly an outside person, but I love to rest outside, and lay on our hammock in the back yard. It is so relaxing and it allows me to speak to the Father. In the hammock, in order to be in balance, you have to lie in the center of the hammock. The hammock must be balanced, so you won't fall and be off centered. Our lives function the same way. We are off balance when we fail to place the Father at the center. When we allow distractions and negative thoughts to enter our minds we are off balance with our Father. We have to remain centered in the Father to hear from God and receive His word. In order to operate in His plans, we must activate wisdom and His presence. We must stand and affirm His word, and stay rooted and grounded. The Father must be our daily source. We must place God first on our agenda for the day. He yearns for us to make Him first. He wants to be the most famous person in our lives. When we choose to place Him in the center, He will share His treasures and open up Heaven for us.

Prayers and Reflections

Lord, we thank you for our angels that you command on our behalf, may they bring forth Heaven to Earth.

Day 17

Angels on Assignment

We have angels in Heaven that are ready to serve the Father. Our angels are ready to serve based on the commands of the Father. We must also speak the right prayers and decrees that create our world. We all have angels assigned to us that help us to reach our purpose and destiny. We have our loved ones in Heaven that are praying and rooting for us in Heaven. God is waiting on us to decree and place our prayers into the atmosphere. Our declarations are heard in Heaven and we operate from Heaven to bring the blessing to Earth. God must honor His word and be faithful to His word. Our words should always line up with the word of God. Oftentimes, we start with speaking right words, and then, life happens and frustration kicks in and negativity. We stop our blessing from coming forth. We must watch the words we speak and be careful to speak right words. I want to keep my angels busy by delivering my blessings. Our blessings are on the menu waiting for us to access them with prayer and decrees. Our angels are waiting to bring forth the blessing once we utilize our authority and power. Our mouth should be open to activate our blessings, so that our angels can praise and bring forth Heaven to us.

Prayers and Reflections

Thank you, Lord that I am one with you and one with the Holy Spirit within. I walk in the fullness of who I am called to be.

Day 18

The War

War is normally fought between two sides that have opposing views. One of the biggest wars that we face besides injustice, police brutality, crime, murder etc... is the war within ourselves. We face spiritual wars in which our true identity comes against the worldly view. We face doubt, unbelief, rejection, worry, and low self-esteem many things that cause us to not walk in the true identity that we were made to operate in. Our blueprint wasn't made by the world, so it looks nothing like what the world view thinks. Our true success comes from knowing who we are, and having the right attitude to bring it forth. We must fully show up and be true to our God given assignment. Our minds need to be renewed daily by speaking right words, aligning ourselves with watching the right things and being around individuals that will help build us up. We must choose to know God's plan and to seek His presence. We must take a step, and move forward towards our destiny. Our thirst for the quest of purpose and destiny must be greater than the fear. Our greatest fear should be to not walk in complete agreement with the blueprint of Heaven. We should not want to leave this Earth and not have truly lived, and walked in purpose. Many have gone to their graves and have not truly lived and walked in purpose. We must look ahead and not behind because, we are made to be overcomers. We are made to win. The Victory has already been won by our Father. Our minds have to be fine-tuned to know that victory is ours and the only one that can stop us from winning is us. No one can stop the purpose that God has called each of us to walk in. Our biggest deficit is what we don't know, and what we can't see. Our Father sees and knows all, and we have to trust the process.

Lord, may we soar to new heights and receive the full inheritance of the kingdom.

Day 19

Soar

Eagles are powerful birds and they soar above. They are made unique to fly high above all the other birds. An Eagle signifies freedom and courage. When you are anointed, you carry greater weight, and go through more warfare. The full promise comes from the testing and trials. The process makes you rooted and grounded in the Father. The word fully lives within and you carry the word with you. When you operate from the origin that the Father created you to operate from you multiply, advance and operate in creativity from above. You operate and dwell in the creative nature of Heaven. You can soar above the rest like the eagles, because you are operating from the reserved seat of Heaven. You have a clear concise understanding of purpose and you know how to unlock doors. Nothing external can operate above you unless you give it power. We must operate from a feeling of strength and boldness and eradicate fear from our lives. Other animals fear the eagle, but the eagle doesn't fear the other birds. It knows that it can soar higher and the other animals will suffocate once it reaches a certain height. God wants us to soar above and advance to a place of divine excellence. He wants us to operate and soar from the place of Heaven, where He called us to operate from. We are fully powerful when we operate from the place of knowing and purpose. We are meant to soar, prosper, and excel... for we are citizens of the kingdom.

Daily Spark Plug

Look Ahead

There is always a blessing in your obedience. Your obedience opens doors, and produces a greater harvest. You are made to set trends, change atmospheres, and walk in power. Being obedient is an important key to your success!

Prayers and Reflections

Lord, may every position you have chosen me for be activated in my life, and may I walk in it fully and boldly.

Day 20

Chosen

When we don't know our true identity, we operate in a false identity. When we don't truly know who we are, we operate at a deficit. We don't know how truly powerful and special we are. Each of us are created in God's image, and we are created with a purpose. You are chosen and called according to God's divine purpose. With God, our future and past are the same. He writes the ending before He adds all of the journey. The journey fits inside of our story. The word says that the steps of a good man are ordered by the Father. When we let the Holy Spirit guide us, we are able to access truth and the divine path. God chose us before we were formed in the womb. He knew exactly who we would become, and how we would arrive. He chose us to bring glory to the world through our gifts and purpose. There are certain gifts that are activated in us that we must be stretched to access. We must gain wisdom to know that many things are hidden within for us to discover. God chose me as a writer and a prophet before I knew that is who I was. You are also chosen to do great things in your life. You are chosen to change the lives around you for His glory. Today, know that God chose you and created you to stand out and be great within.

Prayers and Reflections

Lord, we know that you are the God who makes all things possible. We know that our hope and trust is in you and everything that belongs to us shall come forth.

Day 21

Come Back

All of us love to watch sports, and we have a certain team that we are rooting for to win. Oftentimes, we get upset when our team is not winning. A great coach always said, "There is still time to win as long as there is time on the clock." God knows that He created us to win, and as long as we reside on Earth we have a purpose to fulfill. Sometimes, it may look like we are not going to win or obtain our purpose. Our situation looks dim, and we are not headed in the right direction. Our Father is a God of now and comeback. He has never lost a fight, or battle and His track record is perfect. He is waiting on us to access Him and ask for help. God is waiting to provide us with insight, wisdom, and would love to change our situation. Our Father can change our situation at a moment's notice. It doesn't take Him any time to turn the impossibilities into possibilities. God has a plan A and He doesn't need a B. God has Heavenly insight and knows exactly how to place us on the right track to win. Our comeback time is now. The pain that you are going through shall be used for your good. God is the turnaround, the way-maker, the miracle worker and the winner of the game. He will allow our delays to be turned around into our come-back moment. It is come-back time, it is our season to receive and walk in the sudden blessings and momentum of Heaven.

Daily Spark Plug

Look Ahead

Always give your best in everything you do. Our output represents the Father and ourselves. Our rewards are not from man. Our rewards and gifts come from above.

Jesus says that "Every branch that does not bear fruit He prunes, that it may bear more fruit"

John 15:2

Day 22

Pruning

Often times, things in our life don't mean us any good. They hinder our walk or don't add to who we are. Those dead areas must be pruned or removed from our life. The act of pruning is the act of taking away the dead areas of the plant. After plants are pruned, they can grow stronger and bigger— we have to be pruned as well. The layers of hurt, pain, unbelief, and all the areas that mean us no good have to be pulled away. The Father must heal us of the insecurities within. One touch of God's healing, and we can be made whole again. Two things that keep us from prospering is our mind and our thirst for God. We must focus on the things above, and thirst after the things of God. Only when we walk in the promises and know who we are can we fully operate in the fullness of our true identity. Our full power and purpose is so powerful when we allow God to operate in us. The pruning and tearing away allows us to grow and be grounded. We can't take extra baggage with us on our journey. We can't heal others, if we too need healing. Our crushing, pruning and molding is necessary to become fully effective in our life. If our leaves are dead, we have to be pruned, so we can grow and expand again. The pruning helps to release us into destiny, so we can help others to be released.

"No weapon formed against you shall prosper, and every tongue which raises against you in judgment you shall condemn."

Isaiah 54:17

Day 23

We Are Covered

Things have totally changed in our world. When we go outside and to stores, we must cover up with a mask. Just like we cover ourselves with the mask, we must also cover our family and loved ones in prayer. Jesus is essential in our everyday lives. God's word must stay in our hearts, and we must pray His word and protection over us daily. He is our daily covering and food. We must clothe our minds with His words and renew our hearts with His word. Our homes should be covered with prayer and our children as well. We must impart right words and speak bold prayers over ourselves. Our mouths must be used to bring blessing and covering to our nation and home. When we understand that God provides a covering to His children and that He is faithful to watch over us and His word. We understand that we must not fear, but our trust must be in man. There are many acts of injustice that we hear about daily. When we cover ourselves in prayer, we know that we are protected from harm and danger by the Father. We are citizens of the kingdom, and we follow and live in kingdom. Lord, we thank you for dominion for Heaven to invade Earth. We make you our haven of safety and covering daily. Thank you, Lord that you cover us and you operate in us daily.

"But thanks be to God! He gives us victory through our Lord Jesus Christ."

1 Corinthians 15:57

Day 24

The Mountain

God sees the fork in the road and is aware of everything that tries to hinder you from moving ahead. God is able to adjust our thoughts when we feed our mind with His word. When your mind is aligned with God's plan; his visions and dreams are released to us. God will feed us with wisdom, divine encounters, divine thoughts, and clarity. He will show us how to access the mountains and place the right people in our pathway. He can adjust our now to meet the demand and plans of Heaven. He can activate your dream life again, and every dead area in your life can live again. You will begin to envision life and expect big again. The mountain is a place of higher, enlargement, and experience of truth. It is a place where you wave the flag of victory, because you win and have victory. God longs for us to have mountain top experiences. He longs for us to unlock the treasures within, so our story can coincide with Heaven's book. There will be people that God will place in your life that will be your angels to help catapult you to the mountain. The journey gets tough sometimes, but when we reach our destination, the destiny is fully worth it. We can appreciate our journey, because we can now help others assigned to us shine. There is peace, and victory on the mountain, and we are truly powerful when we operate from the top looking down.

"If my people, who are called by my name, will humble themselves and pray and seek my face and turn from their wicked ways, I will hear from Heaven and heal their land."

2 Chronicles 7:14

Day 25

Change Is Here

There is a great song by the late Otis Redding "Change Gone Come" It is a beautiful song that speaks about needed change in our world. Over the decades, we have witnessed prejudice, injustice, hate, police brutality and corruption in this world. We are aware that it is now time for change. We now know that we must become awakened to the truth. Our world needs Jesus Christ. When we operate according to God's principles, we experience Heaven. The change our world need is God's presence operating in each of us. The glory of God needs to invade our Earth. The creator is the giver and taker of life. We should not see any human blood on the hands of others. We need the character of God and reflection of the Father to invade this nation. Our nation needs to be injected with peace, love, sowing, hope, truth, respect, humility and honor. We need the character of the Father to come alive on Earth. We need to see love and the act of love live within each of us. This nation has many things that have remained hidden, but God will bring it to the fore-front. We need the hand of God to invade Earth and bring forth His perfect divine plan. Only then, will we begin to see true change. The hearts of our leaders must reflect the Father and not pride and power. The hearts of the people must also turn to the Father. Change is here, whether we like it or not, and our Father is King. His perfect plans shall prevail and He shall reign.

Daily Spark Plug

Words Have Power

You are powerful, your words and thoughts are meant to create the world around you. Let the words of Heaven come forth from your mouthpiece daily. Speak life over your business, family, and friends. Think about what you are saying and thinking. Let your thoughts reflect the plans and blueprint of your life. Only when you walk in true purpose… are you fulfilled!

He said to me "Prophesy to these bones and say to them," Dry bones hear the word of the Lord."

Ezekiel 37:4

Day 26

Dry Bones

Bones are the structure and alignment of the body. In the spiritual, when something is out of alignment, it is stagnant or dormant. It doesn't mean that it will not live again, but it needs wind, and the word to come alive. What bones are you currently seeing in your life that have died? There are dreams that need to live again, and need the breath of God. These bones can live again, if we begin to decree and speak life into the atmosphere. Ezekiel in the Holy Bible spoke to the dry bonds, and the wind began to come back into the bones, so they could live. Today, speak to the dead area of your life that has dried up and appear useless. Speak life, and decree life over your marriage, your purpose, your children, and every area of your life that needs the wind of God. I decree that the dead areas of your life shall live again and not die. That the Ruach of God shall cause them to live again and the wind shall be applied to those areas. God wants us to utilize our power within to speak to the bones, and the mountains in our life that seem like they are dead. You can activate Heaven with your voice and the sound when you walk in the presence. Today, know that your dreams, and visions shall live and come into full manifestation. Your destiny shall come forth, and be birth fully, and you shall see the full manifestation of destiny and purpose in your life. The bones that was once dead, we speak life, a mighty wind and a wave of Heaven that filtrates every bone that it shall live and have movement. Every stagnant area of your life, we declare shall move and flow in fullness. I prophesy that fear shall be turned into liberation and wholeness. Everything that was once broke, shall be made whole.

"Many are the plans in a person's heart, but it is the Lord's purpose that prevails."

Proverbs 19:21

Day 27

Beauty in the Pain

In life, we will see storms, trials, and we will experience triumphs. It matters how we look at our pain. There is always beauty and a lesson that you will experience from the pain. It matters how we view our Father. He has everything we need. The trials may be testing your endurance, because on the other side of the pain, a different and a greater door will open. You have to live and expect God to bless you as His sheep. He loves His sheep and He will catapult you to help reach your goals and His plans. He knows exactly how to get His plans to coincide with Heaven on Earth. Cancel the worry and begin to ask God to show you the sunshine in your pain. If you trust in the Father, He shall keep His word and you shall see sunshine, beauty, and triumph in your life. The purpose the Father called you to… is birthed during your pain. We call them birthing pains. Just like you have a physical birth, you also go through spiritual births. The birth is meant to stretch you and bring forth purpose in your life. Your testimony is birthed in the pain. One day, you will be able to understand that pain is necessary so destiny can prevail.

The Lord bless and keep you, the Lord make his face to shine on you and be gracious to you; the Lord turn his face toward you and give you peace."

Numbers 6:24-26

Day 28

The Blessing

In the Jewish culture, the tradition is that the children and family every week are blessed by the head of the home. The Father has a celebration in which he speaks blessings over his children and wife. The tradition allows the blessing to flow from the head to the rest of the family. This important ritual is important, because it imparts a blessing over the family. The tongue is so powerful, and we must watch our words. The tongue has power to build and to tear down. Once words are released, they can't be taken back. Oftentimes, when we use our tongues to tear down, there is pain attached to the words released. Now, healing must take place. One word can cause someone's day to change, and someone's blessing to come forth. That one word of encouragement can help catapult someone in the right direction. How are you using your sword today? Your words are a weapon that we use to pray, encourage, and create. Words can also cause disappointment, discouragement, and strife. We should always use our words to build up, and show the light of Christ. You are a destiny builder, and your words help create destiny. Each of us have the capability to add blessings to help create our destiny. We also have the ability to help shape others destiny as well. Speak life over yourself, your business, and this nation— the world needs more blessings added.

Daily Spark Plug

Pain to Purpose

In life, we will have pains and disappointment. We must never allow the pains of life to poison our thoughts and plans. What is behind is gone, and what is ahead shall be great. There is always a blessing that comes out of the pain. Your destiny is calling!

"Be kind to one another, tenderhearted, forgiving one another, as God in Christ forgave you."

Ephesians 4:32

Day 29

Forgiveness is Impt.

Oftentimes, we become offended by things people do to us, or do to cause us pain. Once someone causes us pain and harm, the event can't be undone. There is normally pain that becomes attached and a rehearsal of the event. When you go through the pain, it is sometimes hurtful, and unbearable, but there is a lesson and a blessing. We must learn to let go of unforgiveness, so we can heal. We must learn to look ahead to our blessings, and not to what lies behind. Healing from the pain and hurt is a process… don't get me wrong. It is a hard, and sometimes a lengthy process. We must let go of the unforgiveness, because it can hinder our blessing, and our purpose. The enemy loves to use those around us to invoke havoc to stop purpose. What the enemy may have used to cause pain and havoc our Father will use for a blessing. This blessing will become your testimony. We should look to our Father to help us to forgive. Secondly, we should pray for the person that hurt us. Lastly, we must move ahead and rehearse what God says and not what man has done to us. Forgiveness is necessary to move forward, but reconciliation is optional. We can still forgive and find peace and move forward in love. Today, choose forgiveness so that your prayers and purpose is not hindered. Remember your blessings are held up because of unforgiveness. Let the Father be the judge who knows all and sees all. When you forgive, you reflect the Father's heart and your reflection resembles Heaven.

"Call unto me, and I will answer thee, and show thee great and mighty things, which thou knowest not."

Jeremiah 33:3

Day 30

Re-Routed

When we miss a turn on the roadway, our GPS will reroute us to the correct direction. We also have a spiritual GPS in the Holy Spirit. The Holy Spirit is there to comfort, route us, and protect us from danger. We have full access to the Holy Spirit, and we carry the presence with us everywhere we go. We must activate and listen to the Spirit that is within. Sometimes, we miss our assignment, because we are distracted or become sidetracked. Our Father knows exactly how to get us back on track with His plans. He knows that right people, and He can line up the right occurrences to line up with His plans. He is an intentional Father. He knows exactly what needs to be done to get His sheep on the right path. The route the Father will have us to take may not coincide with our plans. He knows best, and He knows the quickest route. He knows every turn we must take, and exactly what we will encounter during the journey. As long as you live, your story is still being written. The journey that leads to the end is the dash in-between the dates of existence and death. We must remember to pray daily about our assignment for the day. We must take the Holy Spirit with us and activate our Spiritual GPS. We need the Holy Spirit to keep us on track and get us there on time. Someone is waiting for you to fulfill destiny in order to help them. Remember, our Father is never late, and He is always on time. When we access our Heavenly plans there is no plan B only Plan A. Plan A is always perfect, on time and in accordance to the kingdom laws.

Daily Spark Plug

Sowing

We should always open our hearts to give a smile, a hug, and bless others. Always give with a cheerful heart. There is always a blessing in our giving. It shall be returned back and our true abundance comes from above.

Prayer to Ignite

Lord, thank you that we belong to you, and we are your sheep. We are your sheep that hear your instruction daily. We acknowledge you as our savior and Lord. We declare your divine wisdom of your perfect plans over our life. It shall manifest and come forth. We pray for wisdom, strength, and daily clarity. We thank you for we know that we have the intuition of Heaven to carry forth your plans.

Lord, we thank you that our life shall reflect heaven. Your purpose shall come forth and prevail. We trust and hope in you daily. We know that your plans are perfect and just. We declare the perfect momentum of Heaven to collide over our life and family. We acknowledge that the energy, and surge of Heaven shall be our portion.

<u>tespeaks.com</u>

www.ingramcontent.com/pod-product-compliance
Lightning Source LLC
Chambersburg PA
CBHW071413290426
44108CB00014B/1804